Ducks at a distance

a waterfowl identification guide

Bob Hines

Must Have Books
503 Deerfield Place
Victoria, BC
V9B 6G5
Canada

ISBN 9781773238814

DUCKS
AT A
DISTANCE

A WATERFOWL IDENTIFICATION
GUIDE

Ducks at a Distance

By Bob Hines
DEPARTMENT OF THE INTERIOR
U.S. Fish and Wildlife Service

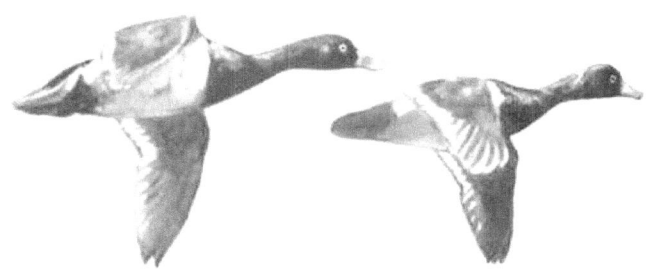

Identification is Important

Identifying waterfowl gives many hours of enjoyment to millions of people. This guide will help you recognize birds on the wing—it emphasizes their fall and winter plumage patterns as well as size, shape, and flight characteristics. It does not include local names.

Recognizing the species of ducks and geese can be rewarding to birdwatchers and hunters—and the ducks.

Hunters can contribute to their own sport by not firing at those species that are either protected or scarce, and needed as breeders to restore the flocks. It can add to their daily limit; when extra birds of certain species can be taken legally, hunters who know their ducks on the wing come out ahead.

Knowing a mallard from a merganser has another side: gourmets prefer a corn-fed mallard to the fish duck.

What to Look For

Differences in size, shape, plumage patterns and colors, wing beat, flocking behavior, voice, and habitat —all help to distinguish one species from another.

Flock maneuvers in the air are clues. Mallards, pintails, and wigeon form loose groups; teal and shovelers flash by in small, compact bunches; at a distance, canvasbacks shift from waving lines to temporary V's.

Closer up, individual silhouettes are important. Variations of head shapes and sizes, lengths of wings and tails, and fat bodies or slim can be seen.

Within shotgun range, color areas can be important. Light conditions might make them look different, but their size and location are positive keys. The sound of their wings can help as much as their calls. Flying goldeneyes make a whistling sound; wood ducks move with a swish; canvasbacks make a steady rushing sound. Not all ducks quack; many whistle, squeal, or grunt.

Although not a hard and fast rule, different species tend to use different types of habitat. Puddle ducks like shallow marshes and creeks while divers prefer larger, deeper, and more open waters.

Flock Pattern   Silhouette   Color Areas   Sound

Eclipse Plumage

Drake: Spring Plumage

Hen

Drakes Emerging from Eclipse

Drake: Full Eclipse

Most ducks shed their body
feathers twice each year.
Nearly all drakes lose their
bright plumage after mating, and for
a few weeks resemble females. This
hen-like appearance is called the
eclipse plumage. The return to
breeding coloration varies
in species and individuals of each
species. Blue-winged teal and shovelers may
retain the eclipse plumage until
well into the winter.

Wing feathers are shed only once
a year; wing colors are always
the same.

Drake: Fall Plumage

Puddle Ducks

Puddle ducks are typically birds of fresh, shallow marshes and rivers rather than of large lakes and bays. They are good divers, but usually feed by dabbling or tipping rather than submerging.

The speculum, or colored wing patch, is generally irridescent and bright, and often a telltale field mark.

Any duck feeding in croplands will likely be a puddle duck, for most of this group are sure-footed and can walk and run well on land. Their diet is mostly vegetable, and grain-fed mallards or pintails or acorn-fattened wood ducks are highly regarded as food.

Feeding   Takeoff

Mallard

Length—24"
Weight—2¾ lbs.

Eclipse Drake

Hen

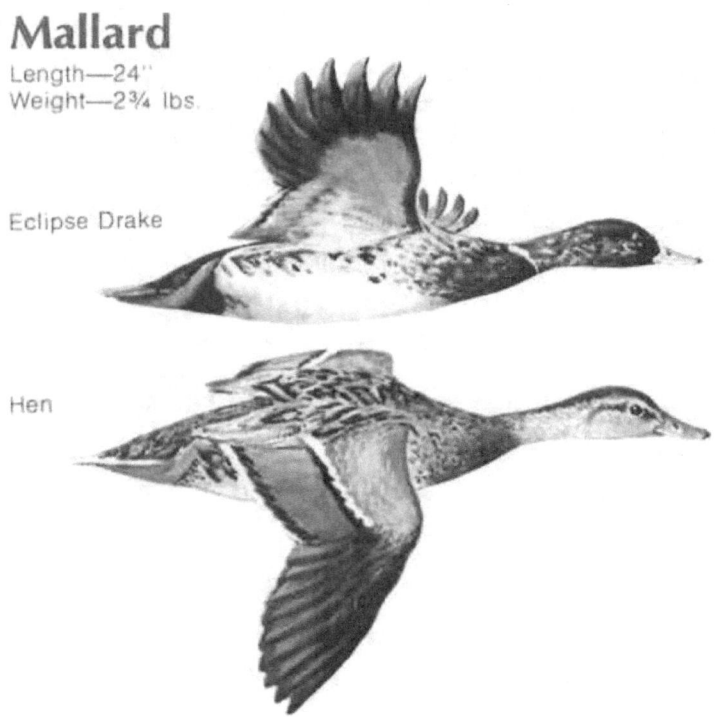

The mallard is our most common duck, found in all flyways. The males are often called "greenheads." The main wintering area is the lower Mississippi basin, and along the gulf coast, but many stay as far north as open waters permits.

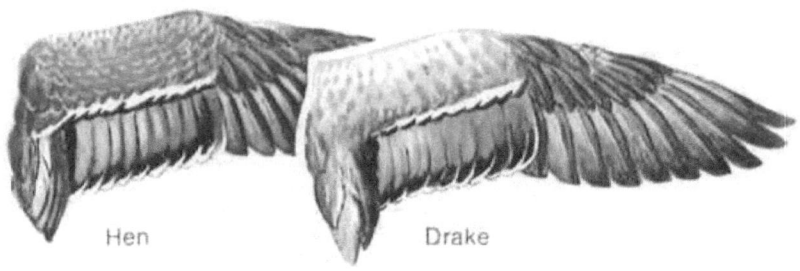

Hen

Drake

Drake

Drake

Hen

Flocks often feed in early
morning and late afternoon in
nearby harvested fields,
returning to marshes and
creeks to spend the night.

The flight is not particularly
rapid. Hens have a loud *quack;*
the drake's voice is a
low-pitched *kwek-kwek.*

Drake

Hen

Typical Flock Pattern

Pintail

Length—26''
Weight—1¾ lbs.

Eclipse Drake

Hen

These ducks use all four flyways, but are most
plentiful in the west.

They are extremely graceful and fast fliers, fond of
zig-zagging from great heights before leveling
off to land.

The long neck and tail make them appear longer
than mallards, but in body size and weight
they are smaller.

Hen   Drake

Drake

Drake

Hen

They are agile on land and often feed in grain fields. The drakes whistle; the hens have a coarse *quack*.

Drake

Hen

Typical Flock Pattern

Gadwall

Length—21"
Weight—2 lbs.

Eclipse Drake

Hen

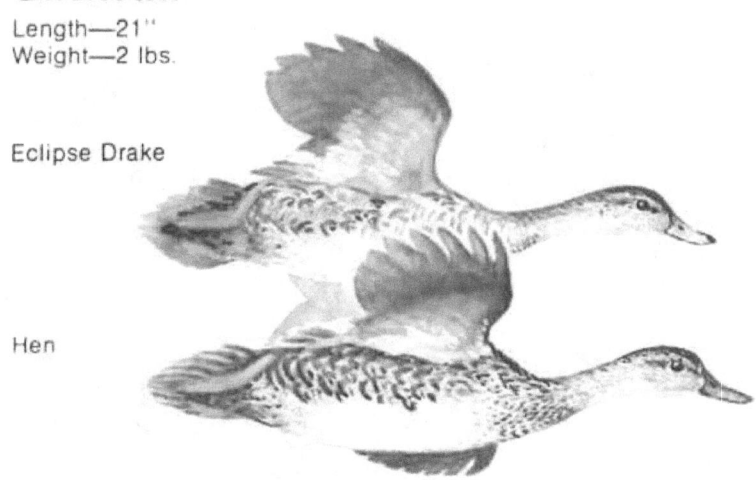

Gadwalls are most numerous in the Central Flyway, but not too common anywhere. They are often called "gray mallards" or "gray ducks." They are one of the earliest migrants, seldom facing cold weather.

They are the only puddle ducks with a white speculum.

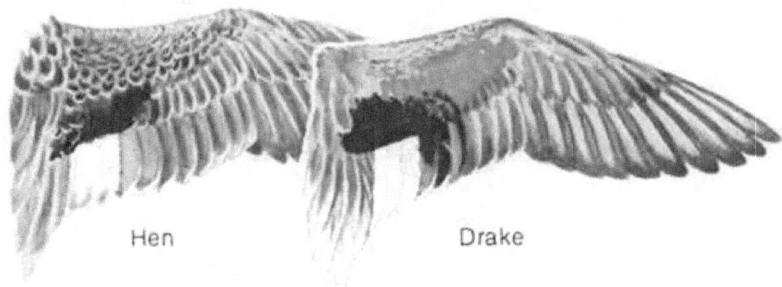

Hen   Drake

Drake

Drake

Hen

Small, compact flocks fly
swiftly, usually in a direct line.
Wingbeats are rapid.

Drakes whistle and *kack-kack;*
hens *quack* like a mallard, but
softer.

Drake

Hen

Typical Flock Pattern

Wigeon

Length—21″
Weight—1¾ lbs.

Eclipse Drake

Hen

These are nervous birds, quick to take alarm. Their
flight is fast, irregular, with many twists and turns. In
a bunched flock, their movements have been
compared to those of pigeons.

When open water is handy, wigeons often
raft up offshore until late afternoon when they
move to marshes and ponds to feed.

Hen   Drake

Drake

Drake

Hen

Drake

Hen

The white belly and forewing are very showy in the air. Drakes whistle; hens have a loud *kaow* and a lower *qua-awk*.

Typical Flock Pattern

Shoveler

Length—19½"
Weight—1½ lbs.

Eclipse Drake

Hen

Shovelers, 'spoonbills' to many, are early migrants, moving out at the first frost. The largest numbers are in the Central and Pacific flyways.

The usual flight is steady and direct. When startled, the small flocks twist and turn in the air like teal.

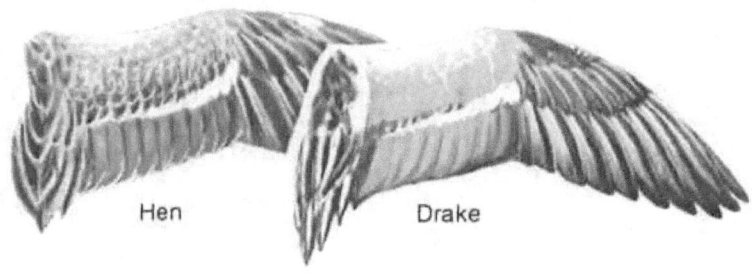

Hen   Drake

Drake

Drake

Hen

They are not highly regarded as table birds, because one third of the usual diet is animal matter.

Drakes call *woh-woh* and *took-took;* the hen's *quack* is feeble.

Drake

Hen

Typical Flock Pattern

Blue-Winged Teal

Length—16"
Weight—15 oz

Hen

Eclipse Drake

Drake

Their small size and twisting
turning flight gives the
illusion of great speed. The
small, compact flocks
commonly fly low over the
marshes, and often take the
hunter by surprise.
They are more vocal than most
ducks—their high-pitched
peeping and nasal quacking is
commonly heard in spring and
to a lesser extent in fall.

These teal are among the first
ducks to migrate each fall, and
one of the last in the spring.

Drake

Hen

Drake

Hen

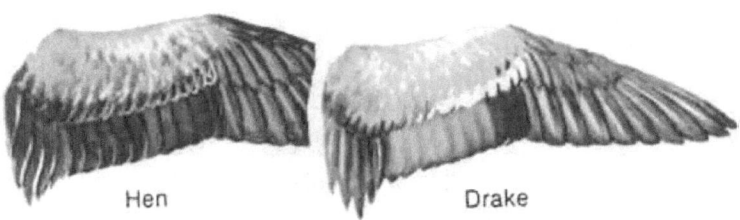

Hen

Drake

Cinnamon Teal

Eclipse Drake

Drake

Blue-Winged Drake

Drake

Hen

Drake

Hen

In the Pacific Flyway, cinnamon teal are far more common than blue-wings. The hens look alike and the habits of both species are similar.

The pale blue forewing patch is the best field mark, as drakes are usually in eclipse until January or longer.

Drakes have a whistling *peep*; hens utter a low *quack*.

Typical Flock Pattern

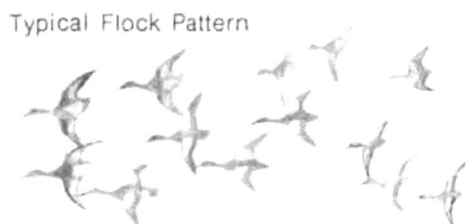

Green-Winged Teal

Length—15 in.
Weight—14 oz.

Eclipse Drake

Hen

Quite hardy—some birds stay as far north as open water is found.

The smallest and one of the most common of our ducks. Their tiny size gives the impression of great speed, but mallards can fly faster. Their flight is often low, erratic, with the entire flock twisting and turning as one unit.

Hen   Drake

Drake

Drake

Hen

They nest as far north as Alaska, and migrate in all four flyways. Early fall drakes are usually still in full eclipse plumage.

Drakes whistle and twitter; hens have a slight *quack*.

Drake

Hen

Typical Flock Pattern

Wood Duck

Length—18 ½ in.
Weight—1 ½ lbs.

Eclipse Drake

Hen

Found in all flyways; most numerous in the Atlantic and Mississippi flyways and fewest in the Central.

They are early migrants; most of them have left the northern States by mid-November.

Frequents wooded streams and ponds; perches in trees. Flies through thick timber with speed and ease and often feeds on acorns, berries, and grapes on the forest floors.

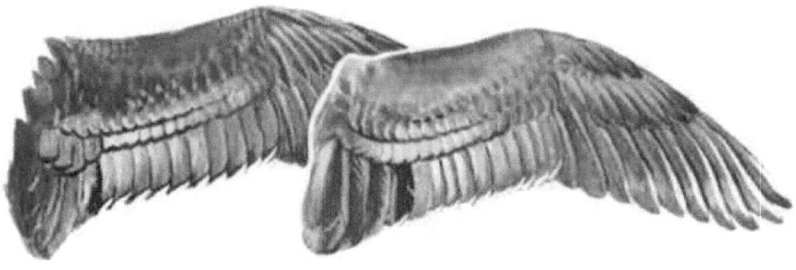

Hen   Drake

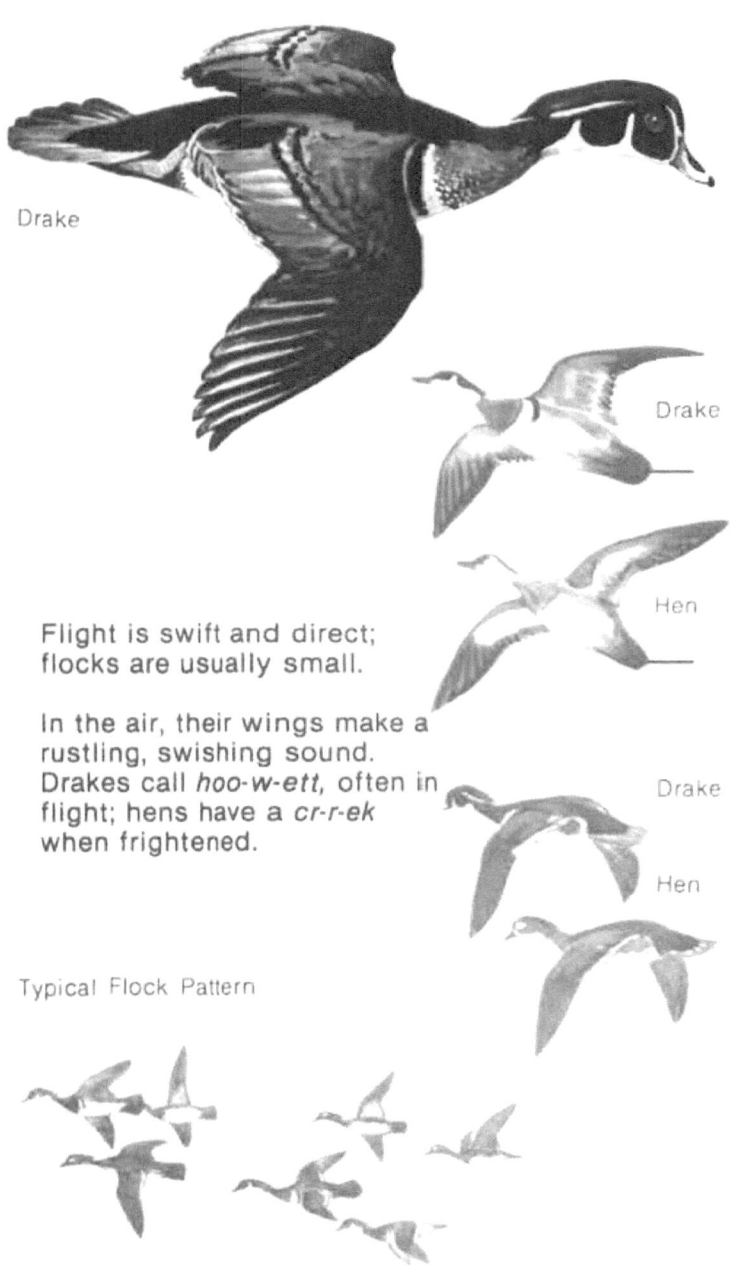

Drake

Drake

Hen

Flight is swift and direct;
flocks are usually small.

In the air, their wings make a
rustling, swishing sound.
Drakes call *hoo-w-ett*, often in
flight; hens have a *cr-r-ek*
when frightened.

Drake

Hen

Typical Flock Pattern

Black Duck

Length—24 in.
Weight—2¾ lbs.

Eclipse Drake

Hen

Drake

Similar Sexes

Typical Flock Pattern

A bird of the eastern States, primarily the Atlantic Flyway and, to a lesser extent, the Mississippi.

Shy and wary, regarded as the wariest of all ducks.

Often seen in company of mallards, but along the Atlantic coast frequents the salt marshes and ocean much more than mallards.

Flight is swift, usually in small flocks.

White wing lining in contrast to very dark body plumage is a good identification clue.

The hen's *quack* and the drake's *kwek-kwek* are duplicates of the mallards.

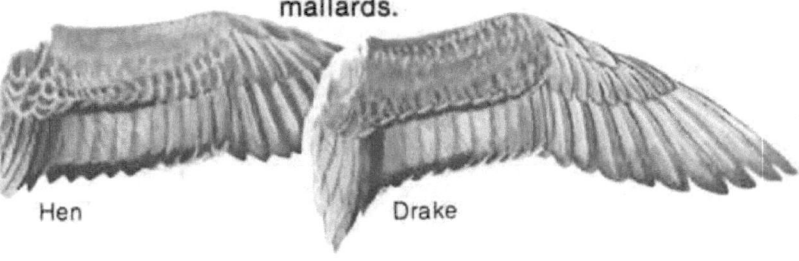

Hen

Drake

Diving Ducks

Diving ducks frequent the larger, deeper lakes and rivers, and coastal bays and inlets.

The colored wing patches of these birds lack the brilliance of the speculums of puddle ducks. Since many of them have short tails, their huge, paddle feet may be used as rudders in flight, and are often visible on flying birds. When launching into flight, most of this group patter along the water before becoming airborne.

They feed by diving, often to considerable depths. To escape danger, they can travel great distances underwater, emerging only enough to show their head before submerging again.

Their diets of fish, shellfish, mollusks, and aquatic plants make then second choice, as a group, for sportsmen. Canvasbacks and redheads fattened on eel grass or wild celery are notable exceptions.

Since their wings are smaller in proportion to the size and weight of their bodies, they have a more rapid wingbeat than puddle ducks.

Takeoff

Feeding

Landing

Canvasback

Length—22 in.
Weight—3 lbs.

Hen

Eclipse Drake

Normally late to start south, canvasbacks migrate in lines and irregular V's.

In feeding areas, compact flocks fly in indefinite formations. Their wingbeat is rapid and noisy; their speed is the swiftest of all our ducks.

Hen   Drake

Drake

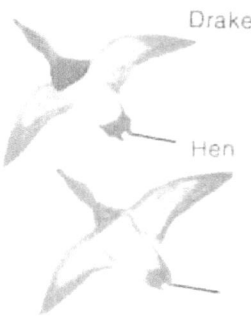

Drake

Hen

Feeding behavior is highly variable. In some areas they feed at night and spend the day rafted up in open waters; in other areas they feed inshore mornings and evenings.

On the water, body size and head shape distinguish them from scaups and redheads.

Drakes *croak, peep,* and *growl;* hens have a mallard-like *quack.*

Drake

Hen

Typical Flock Pattern

Redheads

Length—20 in.
Weight—2 ½ lbs.

Eclipse Drake

Hen

Range coast to coast, with the largest numbers in the
Central Flyway. Migratory flocks travel in V's; move
in irregular formations over feeding areas. Often
found associating with canvasback.

In the air, they give the impression of always being in
a hurry.

Hen

Drake

Drake

Drake

Hen

Usually spend the day in large rafts in deep water; feed morning and evening in shallower sections.

Drakes *purr* and *meow;* hens have a loud *squak,* higher than a hen mallard's.

Drake

Hen

Typical Flock Pattern

Ringneck

Length—17 in.
Weight—2 ½ lbs.

Eclipse Drake

Hen

Similar in appearance to scaups, but more often found in fresh marshes and wooded ponds. In flight, the dark wings are different from the white-edged wings of scaup.

Faint brown ring on drake's neck never shows in the field; light bands at tip and base of bill are conspicuous.

Hen   Drake

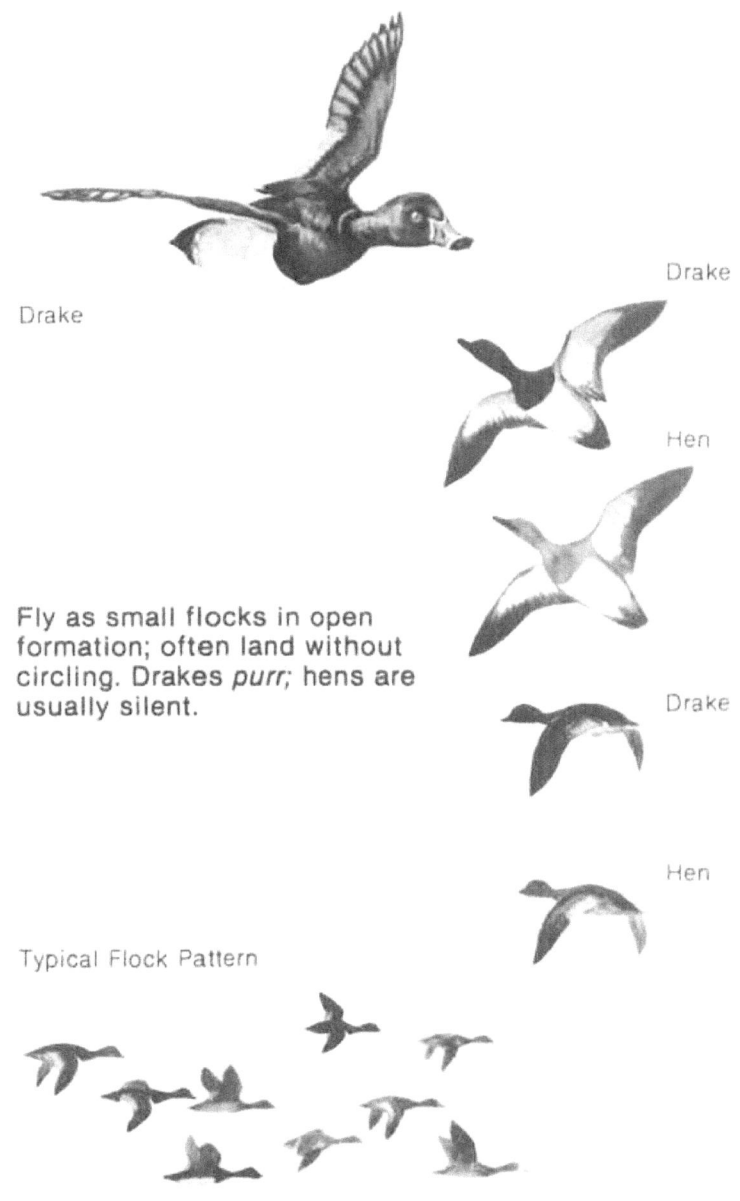

Drake

Drake

Hen

Fly as small flocks in open formation; often land without circling. Drakes *purr;* hens are usually silent.

Drake

Hen

Typical Flock Pattern

Scaup

Greater—Length—18 ½ in.
Weight—2 lbs.

Lesser—Length—17 in.
Weight—1 ⅞

Hen

Eclipse Drake

Except for the wing marks, greater and lesser scaup appear nearly identical in the field.

The light band near the trailing edges of the wings runs almost to the tip in the greater scaup, but only about half way in the lesser.

Greater scaup prefer large open water areas; lesser scaup often use marshes and ponds.

Lesser

Greater

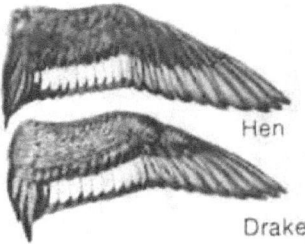

Hen

Drake

Hen

Drake

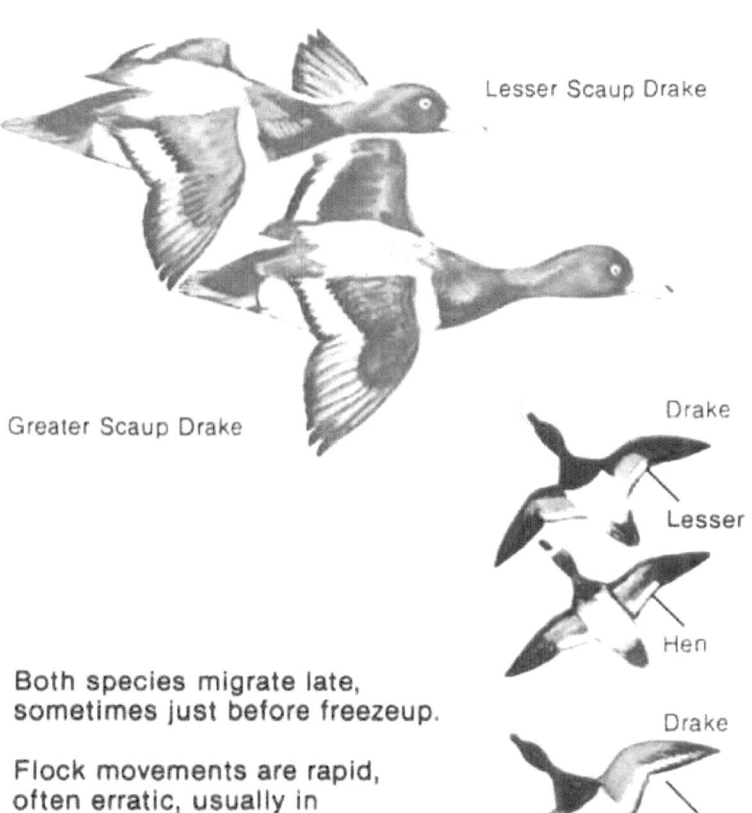

Lesser Scaup Drake

Greater Scaup Drake

Drake

Lesser

Hen

Drake

Greater

Hen

Both species migrate late,
sometimes just before freezeup.

Flock movements are rapid,
often erratic, usually in
compact groups.

Hens are silent; drake lesser
scaup *purr*; drake greater scaup
have a discordant *scaup, scaup*.

Drake

Lesser

Hen

Typical Flock Pattern

Goldeneye

Common—Length—19 in.
        Weight—2 ¼ lbs.

Barrow's—Length—19 in.
        Weight—2¾ lbs.

Hen Both Species

Common Eclipse Drake

These are active, strong-winged fliers moving singly or in small flocks, often high in the air. Distinctive wing-whistling sound in flight has earned the name of whistlers.

Goldeneyes generally move south late in the season; most of them winter on coastal waters and the Great Lakes. Inland, they like rapids and fast water.

Barrow's   Common

Hen   Drake   Hen   Drake

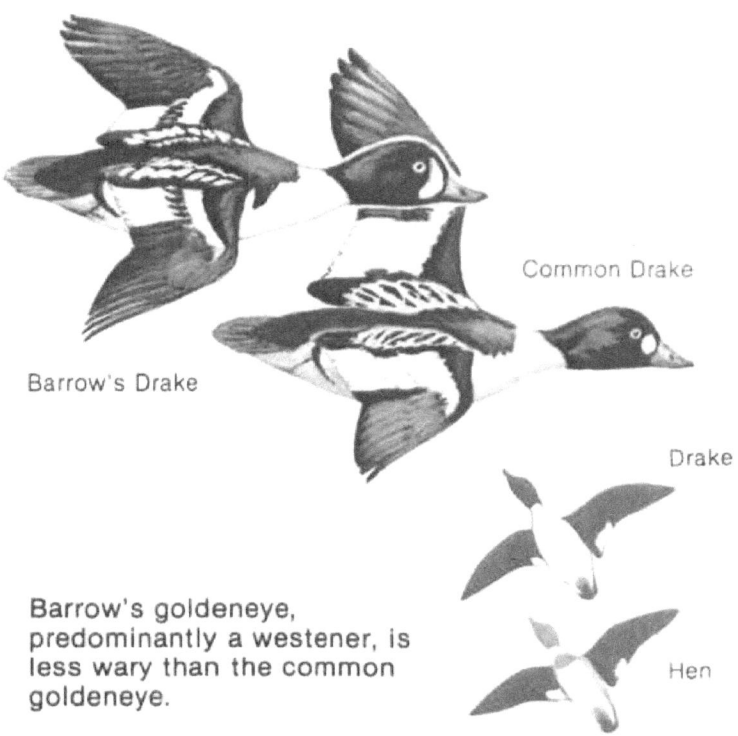

Common Drake

Barrow's Drake

Drake

Barrow's goldeneye,
predominantly a westener, is
less wary than the common
goldeneye.

Hen

Hens of both species are
look-alikes.

Drakes have a piercing
speer-speer—hens a low
quack. Both are usually quiet.

Drake

Hen

Typical Flock Pattern

Bufflehead

Length—14½ in
Weight—1 lb.

Hen

Eclipse Drake

Stragglers migrate south in mid-fall, but the largest numbers move just ahead of freezeup. Most flocks in feeding areas are small—5 or 6 birds, with more hens and immatures than adult drakes.

Very small size, bold black and white color pattern, and low, swift flight are field marks. Unlike most divers, they can fly straight up from a watery takeoff.

Hen   Drake

Drake

Drake

Hen

Largest concentrations are on both seacoasts and along the Gulf of Mexico. Inland, they will remain as far north as open water permits.

Usually silent. Drakes *squeak* and have a guttural note; hens *quack* weakly.

Drake

Hen

Typical Flock Pattern

Ruddy

Length—15½ in.
Weight—1⅓ lbs.

Winter Drake

Hen

The ruddy duck often dives or swims away
from danger rather than flying. When flying, their
small wings stroke so fast they resemble
bumblebees.

Sexes Similar

Summer Drake

Drake

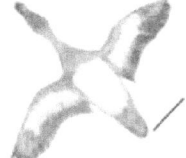

They are early to mid-fall
migrants.

Hen

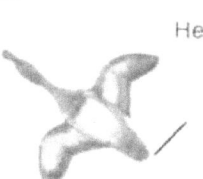

Drakes often cock their tails
upright at an angle, the only
species to habitually do so.

Both hens and drakes are
silent in the fall.

Drake

Hen

Typical Flock Pattern

Red-Breasted Merganser

Length—23 in.
Weight—2 ½ lbs.

Eclipse Drake

Drake

Hen

These birds winter most abundantly in coastal waters, including the Gulf of Mexico, and to a lesser extent, the Great Lakes.

Their flight, strong and direct, is usually low over the water. They are difficult to distinguish in flight from the common merganser.

Voice: Seldom heard.

Drake

Hen

Drake

Hen

Typical Flock Pattern

Hen   Drake

Common Merganser

Length—25½ in.
Weight—2½ lbs.

Eclipse Drake

Drake

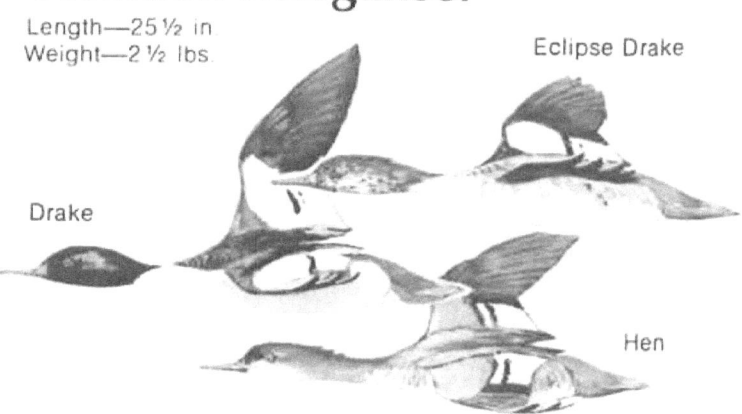

Hen

This species is larger than the red-breasted merganser, and is one of the largest of our ducks. It is one of the last to migrate south, and is more common than the red-breasted merganser on inland waters.

Flocks move in "follow the leader" style, low over the water.

The only call seems to be a startled *croak*.

Drake

Hen

Drake

Hen

Typical Flock Pattern

Hen   Drake

Hooded Merganser

Length—18 in.
Weight—1 ½ lbs.

Eclipse Drake

Drake

Hen

Drake

Hen

Drake

Hen

Often seen in pairs, or very small flocks. Short rapid wingstrokes create an impression of great speed.

Winters in the inland waters of all coastal States; seldom goes to salt water.

Voice: Seldom heard in fall.

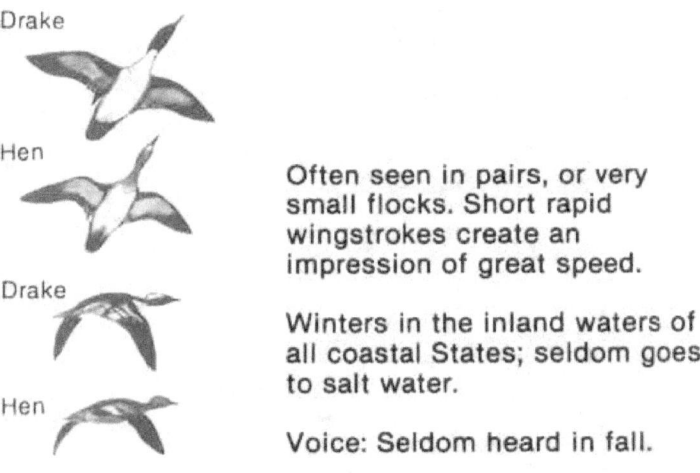

Hen   Drake

Whistling Ducks

Length—18–19 in.
Weight—1¾ lbs.

Fulvous

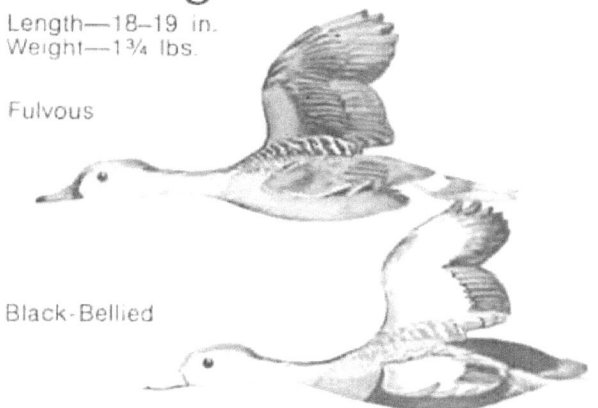

Black-Bellied

The trailing legs and rounded wings of these slow flying ducks makes them look bigger than they are.

Fulvous

Both species are primarily Mexican. In the U.S., the black-bellied is found only in south Texas and Louisiana. The fulvous also occurs there and in Florida with occasional stragglers further north along both coasts and the Mississippi Valley. The fulvous is the more common of the two species in the United States.

Black-Bellied

Sexes are alike. Both species have shrill whistling calls.

Fulvous   Black-Bellied

White-Winged Scoter

Length—21½ in.
Weight—3½ lbs.

Immature

Drake

Hen

The three scoters on these two pages are sea ducks, wintering on open coastal waters. White-wings are among the heaviest and largest of all ducks.

Surf Scoter

Length—19½ in.
Weight—2 lbs.

Immature

Drake

Hen

Like all scoters, these birds move along our coasts in loose flocks, stringing into irregular, wavy lines. Drakes can be distinguished from other scoters by two white patches on their head and the bright color of the bill.

Flight is strong, direct, usually close to the waves.

Black Scoter

Length—19 ½ in.
Weight—2 ½ lbs.

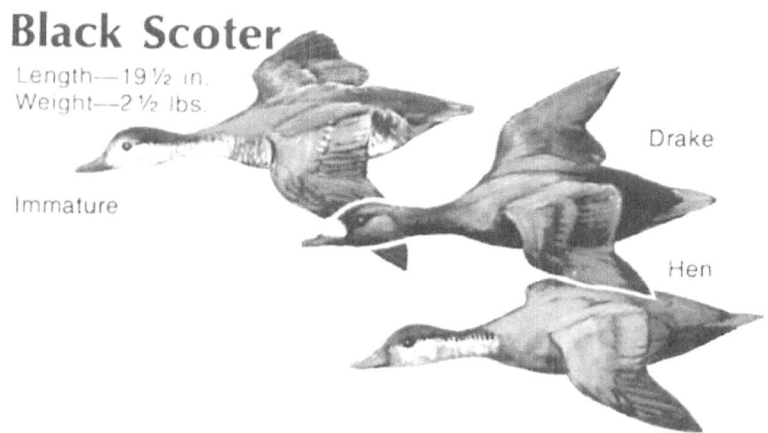

Drake

Immature

Hen

In flight, drakes appear all black except for the flash of the slight gray underwing and the bright yellow swelling at the base of the upper bill.

Scoters feed on mollusks, crabs, and some fish and very little vegetation. They are locally known as "coots."

Common Eider

Length—23 ½ in.
Weight—5 lbs.

Drake

Eclipse Drake

Hen

Thick-necked stocky birds, alternately flapping and sailing in flight; flocks string out in a line, close to the water. Occurs in the United States chiefly along New England coasts and occasionally south to New Jersey.

Other eiders—king, spectacled and Stellar's—occur in Alaska and are not pictured in this guide. King eiders occasionally are found in north Atlantic coastal waters.

Long-tailed Duck

Length—20 ½ in.
Weight—2 lbs.

Winter Drake

Summer Drake

Winter Hen

A slim, brightly plumaged sea duck. Smaller than the scoters or eiders.

Flight is swift and low with constantly changing flock formations. Ranges along both coasts and the Great Lakes.

One of the most vocal of ducks; drakes have a loud pleasant *caloo, caloo,* constantly heard.

Harlequin

Length—17 in.
Weight—1 ½ lbs.

Drake

Eclipse Drake

Hen

Glossy slate-blue plumage enlivened by white stripes and spots give the adult male harlequin a striking appearance. The female resembles a small female scoter. At a distance, both sexes look black. Flight is swift, with abrupt turns. Flocks are small and compact. Ranges both coasts, north from New Jersey and San Francisco. Uncommon.

Swans

Trumpeter—Length—59 in.
     Weight—28 lbs.

Tundra –Length—52 in.
     Weight—16 lbs.

Trumpeter

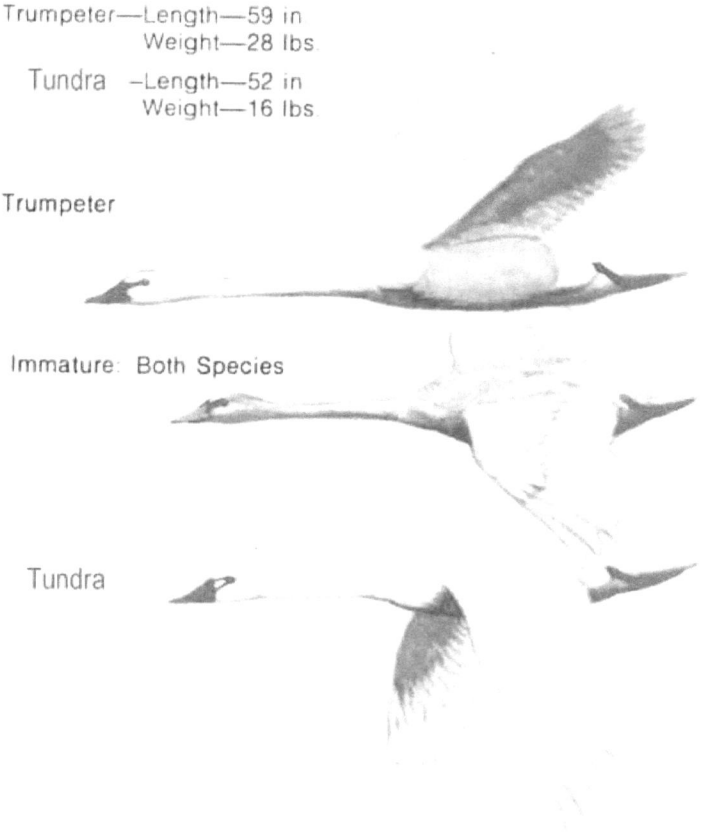

Immature: Both Species

Tundra

Once thought to be rare, trumpeter swans are slowly increasing in Alaska and on western refuges and parks.

Tundra swans are common and increasing. They winter near Chesapeake Bay, San Francisco Bay, Puget Sound and Salton Sea. Occasionally found in fields.

Both species are large with pure white plumage.

Canada Geese

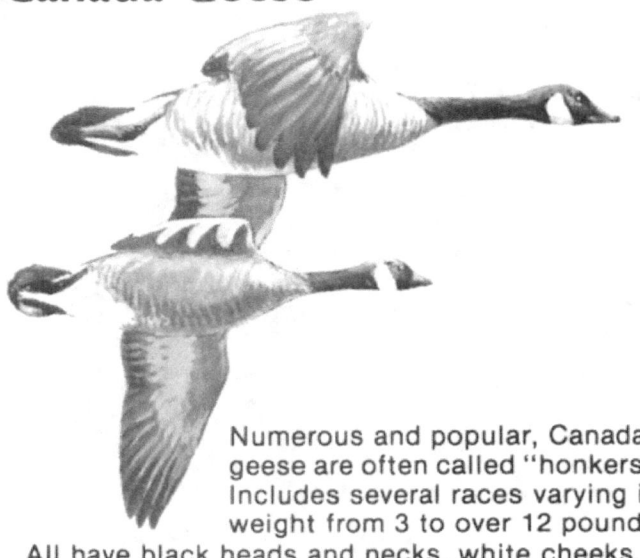

Numerous and popular, Canada geese are often called "honkers." Includes several races varying in weight from 3 to over 12 pounds. All have black heads and necks, white cheeks, similar habitats and voices. Sexes are identical.

Brant

Length—24–25 in.
Weight—3¼–3¾ lbs.

Black Brant

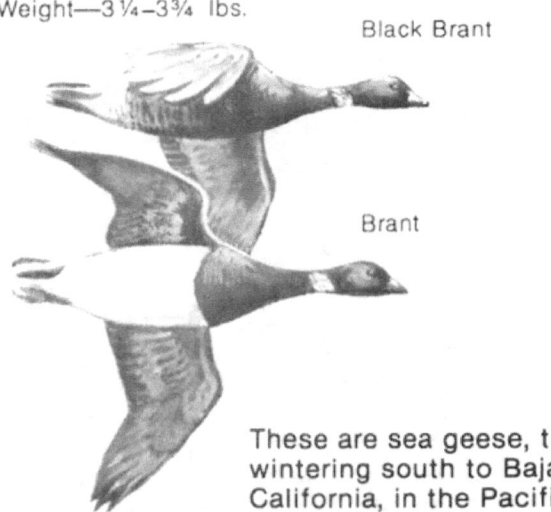

Brant

These are sea geese, the blacks wintering south to Baja, California, in the Pacific. The Atlantic race winters from Virginia northward. Flight is swift, in irregular and changing flock patterns.

Snow Geese

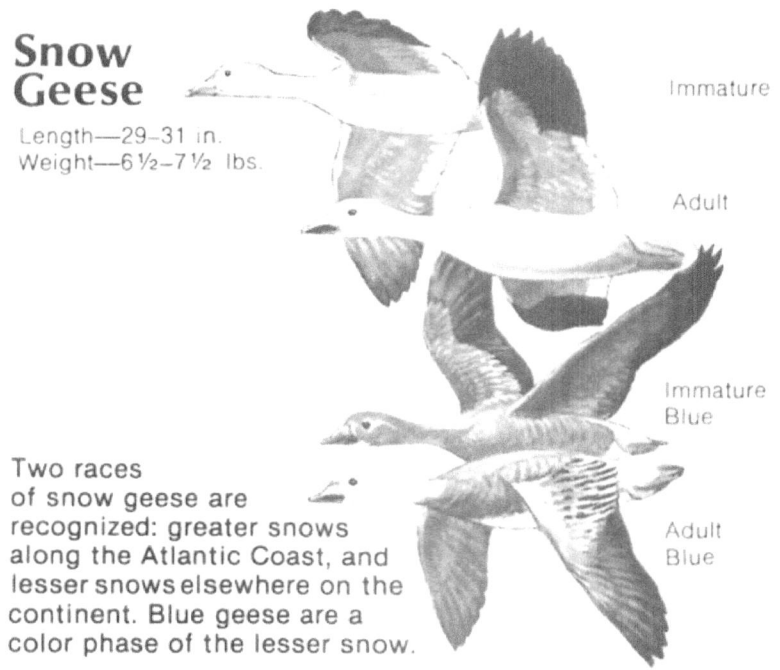

Length—29–31 in.
Weight—6½–7½ lbs.

Immature

Adult

Immature
Blue

Adult
Blue

Two races
of snow geese are
recognized: greater snows
along the Atlantic Coast, and
lesser snows elsewhere on the
continent. Blue geese are a
color phase of the lesser snow.

White-Fronted Geese

Length—29 in.
Weight—6¼ lbs.

Immature

Adult

Migrates chiefly in the Central and Pacific
flyways but also present in the Mississippi.
Rare in the Atlantic Flyway. Appears brownish
gray at a distance. Often called "specklebelly".

Most distinctive characteristic of the V-shaped
flocks is the high pitched call *kow-kow-kow-kow*.

Pintail

Bufflehead

Mallard

Ruddy

Black Duck

Ringneck

Gadwall

Lesser Scaup

Wigeon

Greater Scaup

Shoveler

Goldeneye

Wood Duck

Redhead

Cinnamon
Teal

Canvasback

Blue-Winged
Teal

Hooded
Merganser

Green-Winged
Teal

Red-Breasted
Merganser

Common
Merganser

Trumpeter Swan

Tundra Swan

Canada Goose

Greater Snow Goose

White-Fronted Goose

Lesser Canada Goose

Lesser Snow Goose

Emperor Goose

Black Brant

Brant

Cackling Goose

Ross' Goose

COMPARATIVE SIZES OF WATERFOWL

All birds on these pages are drawn to the same scale.

Harlequin

Long-tailed Duck

Whistling Ducks

Surf Scoter

Common Scoter

White-Winged Scoter

Common Eider

Wetlands Attract Wildlife

There's more than just ducks in our marshes.
Knowing and identifying other birds and animals add
to the enjoyment of being in a blind.

The same sources of food and shelter that draw
waterfowl to ponds and marshes also attract other
forms of wildlife.

Protected species are sometimes more numerous than
ducks or geese.

Money from Duck Stamp sales is used exclusively to
purchase wetlands, preserving areas for ducks, geese,
and all wildlife for the enjoyment and pleasure of
hunters and non-hunters alike.

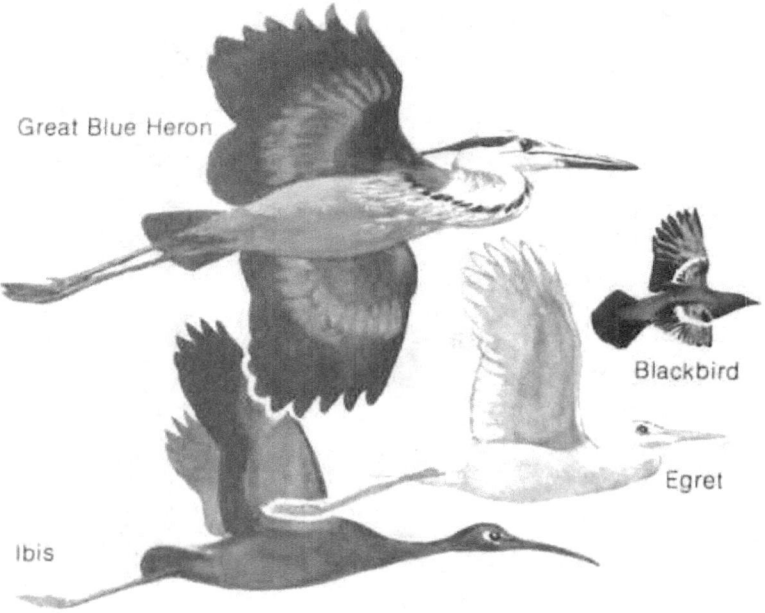

Great Blue Heron

Blackbird

Egret

Ibis

Cormorant

White Pelican

Black Tern

Common Tern

Marsh Hawk

Yellowlegs

Herring Gull

Dowitcher

Grebe

Short-Eared Owl

Administrative Waterfowl Flyways

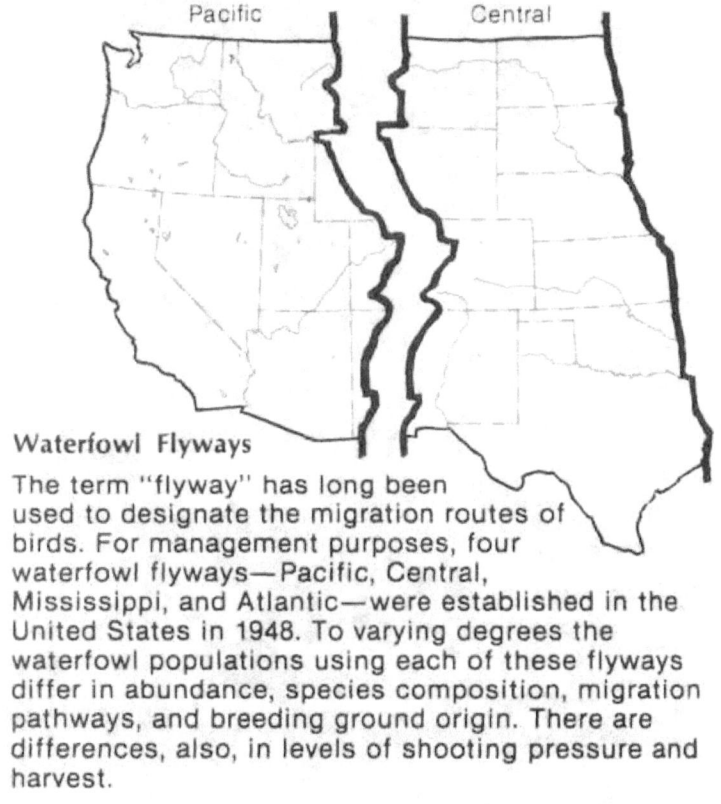

Pacific   Central

Waterfowl Flyways

The term "flyway" has long been used to designate the migration routes of birds. For management purposes, four waterfowl flyways—Pacific, Central, Mississippi, and Atlantic—were established in the United States in 1948. To varying degrees the waterfowl populations using each of these flyways differ in abundance, species composition, migration pathways, and breeding ground origin. There are differences, also, in levels of shooting pressure and harvest.

For the most part flyway boundaries follow State lines. However, the boundary between the Pacific and the Central flyway general follows the Continental Divide.

There are some problems in matching waterfowl migration corridors with flyway boundaries because some species nest and winter in areas that do not occur along a north-south axis. These species cross flyway boundaries during migration. On balance, the present arrangement is useful in that it permits reasonable management of waterfowl. At some future time, it is possible that further rearrangement of boundaries may permit better management of the waterfowl resource.

Mississippi

Atlantic

Flyway Councils

In 1952, Flyway Councils were formed in each of the four flyways. The Council in each flyway is made up of representatives from the wildlife agencies of the States in that flyway—one representative from each State. The Councils study flyway problems, develop waterfowl management recommendations, and generally work closely with the U.S. Fish and Wildlife Service in implementing waterfowl management and research programs.

Washington Department of
FISH and WILDLIFE

www.ingramcontent.com/pod-product-compliance
Lightning Source LLC
Chambersburg PA
CBHW050911120626
46552CB00004B/1517